A Little Schubert

A Little Schubert

Story and Pictures by M. B. GOFFSTEIN

Record by Peter Schaaf

Harper & Row, Publishers

NEW YORK   EVANSTON   SAN FRANCISCO   LONDON

Library of Congress Catalog Card Number: 72-79899
Harpercrest Standard Book Number: 06-022027-9
Trade Standard Book Number: 06-022026-0

FIRST EDITION

To the Schaafs

A Little Schubert

In a cold and snowy town called Vienna,

a short fat young man with a small round nose,

and he did not mind his bare room or his shabby clothes.

But when the cold made his fingers ache,
and he almost could not write his music,
Franz Schubert got up.

He clapped his hands

and stamped his feet.

He made his shabby coattails fly

as he danced to keep warm.

round eyeglasses and curly hair,

lived in a bare little room without a fire.

He was a composer.

Every morning he sat at a little table

and wrote music as fast as it came into his head.

Franz Schubert heard music

when his friends heard nothing,

and Franz Schubert heard music

that no one had ever heard before.

He heard so much music in his head

he could not possibly remember it all.

So Franz Schubert was very busy writing down his music

Here is a record
of five of the twelve dances
called "Noble Waltzes"
that Franz Schubert wrote down
in his little room in Vienna,
around one hundred and fifty years ago.